Bobbi Finds a Forever Home

a true story

First Printing, 2016

ISBN 978-1-63110-243-1

Mira Digital Publishing

174 Chesterfield Industrial Blvd.

Chesterfield MO 63005

www.mirabooksmart.com

For my mother, Miss Dotty,
and for Bobbi,
who continually nourish
my soul with showers of love.

Bobbi is a Maine Coon cat with a mysterious past.

Maine Coon cats can grow very big with long fur and thick fluffy tails. Tufts of fur stick out from the tips of their ears and between the toes of their large paws. They have something called ruffs that look like a lion's mane or a big fur collar.

Maine Coon cats come in many colors. Bobbi's colors look like something good to eat. Her ruff and belly and paws are the color of vanilla ice cream. Her fur is the color of caramel and chocolate. Her pink nose wears a little white dot like a dusting of powdered sugar.

Only Bobbi knows the story of where she came from and how she got to the woods.

Bobbi has scars inside from broken ribs and a broken jaw. Did she get hit by a car? Did a human hurt her? Did she fall out of a tree? Bobbi had no home. She was alone, hurt and hungry. Bobbi knew a secret. She was going to have babies.

Soon she gave birth to two little kittens. Bobbi was born with instincts that let her know how to care for her kittens. She hunted for food for herself so she could be strong and make milk for her kittens.

The forest was a scary place where rain often fell. Thunder boomed and lightning cracked and rain poured from the sky. Bobbi watched out for foxes and hawks that might try to eat her kittens. She kept her kittens hidden, but she was ready to fight anything that might attack them.

She moved her kittens every day looking for a safe and dry place to stay. Moving the kittens was hard work. Bobbi had to move one kitten at a time. She picked up each kitten by its neck and carried it in her mouth to a new hiding place. The kittens learned to go limp and hang quietly when she carried them.

Sometimes Bobbi and her kittens had to sleep outside. Other times they found a barn where they could be warm and dry. Bobbi moved the kittens so often that her teeth wore off parts of their fur and left sores on their necks.

One day Bobbi's sharp nose smelled something tasty. It was meat, but not just any meat – *Chicken*! Her favorite!

She left the kittens sleeping in an old shed and followed the scent. Soon she came to a pretty little blue house that belonged to an old farmer. A lady on the deck was grilling chicken!

Bobbi crept closer to the deck, but kept a safe distance. Living on her own had made her careful of strangers. Yet she smiled her best smile at the lady as if to say, "I LOVE chicken!"

The lady's name was Diana. The farmer was her father and Diana visited him every weekend. Diana said, "Hi cat. You are so pretty. You look like a Maine Coon with your long fur, your big furry paws, and your long fluffy tail. Are you hungry?"

The old farmer shook his cane and said,

"Do NOT feed that cat! It will never leave."

Diana fed Bobbi some chicken anyway.

10

Bobbi thought, "This looks like a good place for my kittens and me to stay. We can sleep under the deck and maybe the lady will feed me more chicken." So one by one Bobbi carried her kittens from the old shed and put them under the deck.

Diana saw that the cat was a good mother. Bobbi fed her kittens until they were round and fat and she washed them every day. She taught them to hunt so they could feed themselves when they got older.

Diana said to herself, "This is such a nice cat that someone will be looking for her." She took a picture of Bobbi and put it in all the stores with a sign that said "Cat Found." She waited and waited, but no one came to get Bobbi.

Diana was worried because she did not want a cat and she did not want any kittens. She lived in an apartment in St. Louis. She did not think an apartment was a good home for a cat. She did not want to share her home with a cat. She did not want to spend her money for cat food or vet bills. She did NOT want to scoop poop. She wasn't even sure she *liked* cats.

Soon the kittens found forever homes, but no one wanted Bobbi. Every weekend Diana visited Bobbi at the old farmer's house in the country. As time passed, Bobbi and Diana grew closer. They sat together on the deck while Diana brushed Bobbi's soft fur and petted her and talked to her. Bobbi purred with happiness and rubbed against her.

She knew something that Diana didn't know yet.

Week after week Diana tried to find someone to take Bobbi. As each person she asked said no, Diana said, "Bobbi, you deserve a better human than this. You deserve someone who will love you."

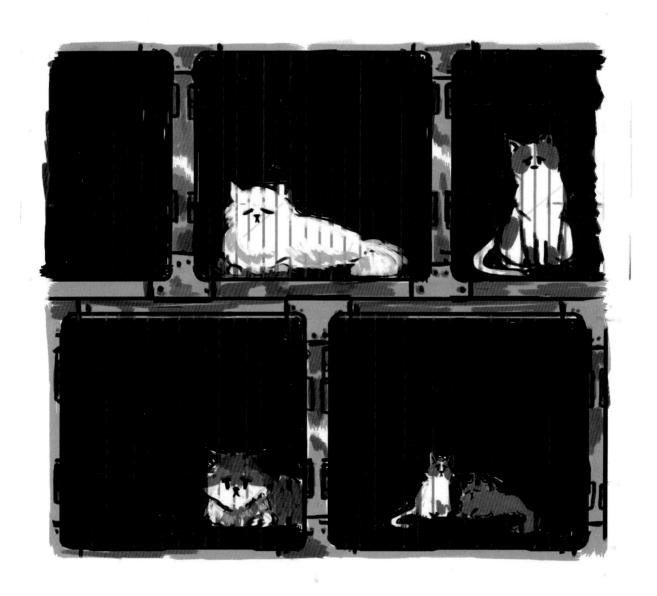

Finally, Diana decided to give Bobbi to a shelter.
She called many shelters looking for one that had room for
Bobbi. But she learned that shelters can't always find homes
for grown cats. The people at the shelters told her that the
unwanted cats might be put down to make room for more cats
at the shelter.

Diana was horrified. She got angry. She cried
out, "No one is going to kill MY cat!"

Her words hung in the air between her and Bobbi. At last Diana
knew what Bobbi knew all along: she loved Bobbi and they
belonged together.

After all, a forever home doesn't have to be in any special
place. A forever home happens when two or more hearts care
for each other. Diana and Bobbi had found a forever home
together.

The Beginning.

Please consider adopting a pet

from your local shelter

or making a donation

to help save a life.